Music Minus One Trumpet
Also suitable for any B♭ Instrument

SIGNATURE SERIES

VOL. 3

6855

And how 'bout this for an interesting fact: This hit of Peggy's, *Why Don't You Do Right?* that she recorded with Benny Goodman's band in 1942 that sold over a million records was originally recorded in 1936 as Weed Smoker's Dream which dealt with a marijuana smoker's reminiscence about lost financial opportunities!

When re-written it became the classic woman's blues song.

So, relax into this swingin' big band minor blues that gives you two keys to play with - E minor and F minor. Towards the end you get a chance to "blow" and it's a fun song to open up and explore!

There's also a great video on YouTube with a fine quartet backing up young Peggy that's well worth watching.

On Ella Fitzgerald's *Every Time We Say Goodbye,* I decided to play it all on flugelhorn for the warmth that's required with this pensive Cole Porter song.

There are two challenges with Every: First, it's in our key of A Major and the lower octave is loaded with the two most difficult notes to play in tune, namely low D and C#! "Lipping" them down from their inherently "sharp" nature is an option but an awkward one. If you have a trigger on your flugelhorn it's fairly easy. (With some practice, of course!)

Enjoy this masterfully orchestrated background and please be patient with yourself when getting into synch with the track in the rubato section.

Ray Charles took this next song *You Don't Know Me* to #2 on the Billboard Hot 100 Chart in 1962. For me, only Ray could take this simple Country song by Eddy Arnold and convey such a deep, message so soulfully!

Take a listen to Ray on YouTube and then imagine yourself singing through the horn and telling the very same story!

The amazing Fred Astaire first introduced Irving Berlin's *Steppin' Out With My Baby* in the 1948 movie Easter Parade. Although Astaire's reputation is primarily as a dancer/actor, he had an uncanny "way with a song". In fact, many of the songwriters of the Great American Song Book openly admired his lyricism, diction and phrasing. It seemed that the grace and elegance so prized in his dancing was reflected in his singing!

Note the "cool" use of the verse as an interlude that leads to a very "hip" piano solo!

I stayed with the Harmon mute throughout to accentuate the intimate quality of this background that is just a rhythm section.

Days Of Wine And Roses is from the 1962 movie of the same name. Henry Mancini teamed up with Johnny Mercer and it received an Oscar for Best Original Song! The best known recording was by Andy Williams.

As you probably have surmised by now, especially if you've acquired any of my previous MMOs, I'm "head over heels" in love with MELODY!

Although. improvisation is to me one of the great avenues of human expression, to take a given melody whether Classical, Jazz, Folk or from The Great American Song Book and render it with my personal phrasing and emotion is one of the most satisfying pleasures of life!

Mancini's melody has just that potential and here again with a world-class rhythm section provided on this track by Irv Kratka the founder and still president of Music Minus One, it was a total delight for me to create. I hope you find it inspiring!

For the last song I chose *God Bless The Child* which Billie Holiday wrote and recorded in 1941. It was inducted into the Grammy Hall Of Fame in 1976.

It brings back a vivid memory in 1960 while on Maynard Ferguson's Band. We were doing an outdoor concert and it may have been the Newport Jazz Festival. Billie Holiday was on the bill and when she finally showed up, sadly, she was in such bad shape that she had to be wheeled out to sing. Despite this tragic overtone, the unmistakable Lady Day voice drenched with only sincere emotions came through crystal clear!

Oh my God, it's 2014 and here I am time-traveling instead of talking about this present and rather unique arrangement of God Bless The Child that allows for a kaleidoscopic (for lack of a better word) journey through this usually introspective and yes melancholy song.

For starters, you'll hear full-bodied cello obbligatos that set a rather haunting tone for my trumpet solo. Then there's a transition into a shouting, brassy big band ensemble that leads to finality with a high note ending!

I wish for you the same kind of enjoyment playing with this album as I experienced creating it.

I'm now offering a complimentary Skype or FaceTime session to help you gain the maximum benefit from this and my other MMOs. You can contact me at bobzottola@naplesjazzlovers.com

All the best!
Bob Zottola
Naples, Florida
www.naplesjazzlovers.com

SIGNATURE SERIES

CONTENTS

ISBN 978-1-941566-96-1

MMO 6855

Lullaby of Birdland

Solo Bb Trumpet

George Shearing
George Weiss

Transcribed by Jeff Helgesen

This page intentionally left blank to facilitate page turns.

Solo Bb Trumpet (Flugelhorn)

When I Fall In Love

Victor Young
Edward Heyman

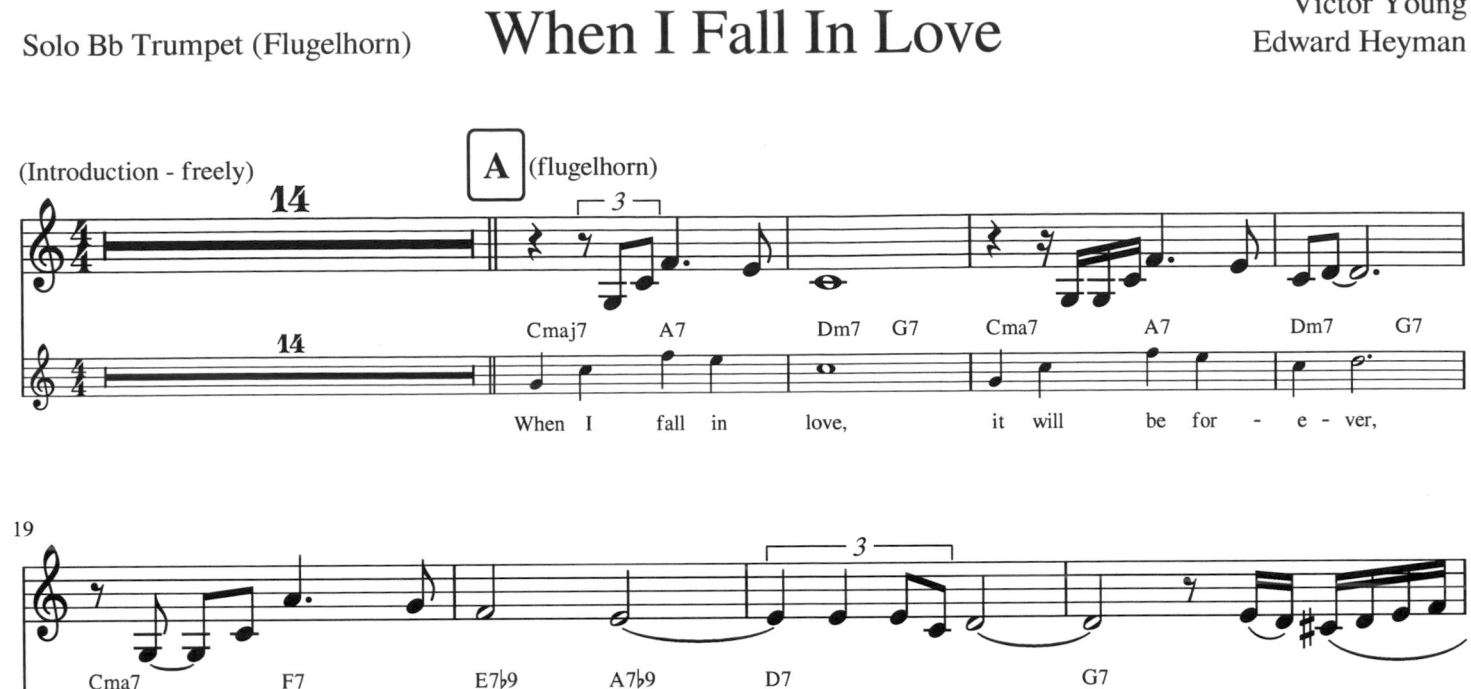

give my heart_____ And the mo-ment I can feel that____ you feel that____ way too, is when I fall in love with you

Transcribed by Jeff Helgesen

Why Don't You Do Right

Solo Bb Trumpet

Joseph McCoy

12

Transcribed by Jeff Helgesen

This page intentionally left blank to facilitate page turns.

Ev'ry Time We Say Goodbye

Solo Bb Flugelhorn

Cole Porter

Transcribed by Jeff Helgesen

This page intentionally left blank to facilitate page turns.

You Don't Know Me

Solo Bb Trumpet

Eddy Arnold
Cindy Walker

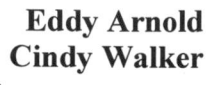

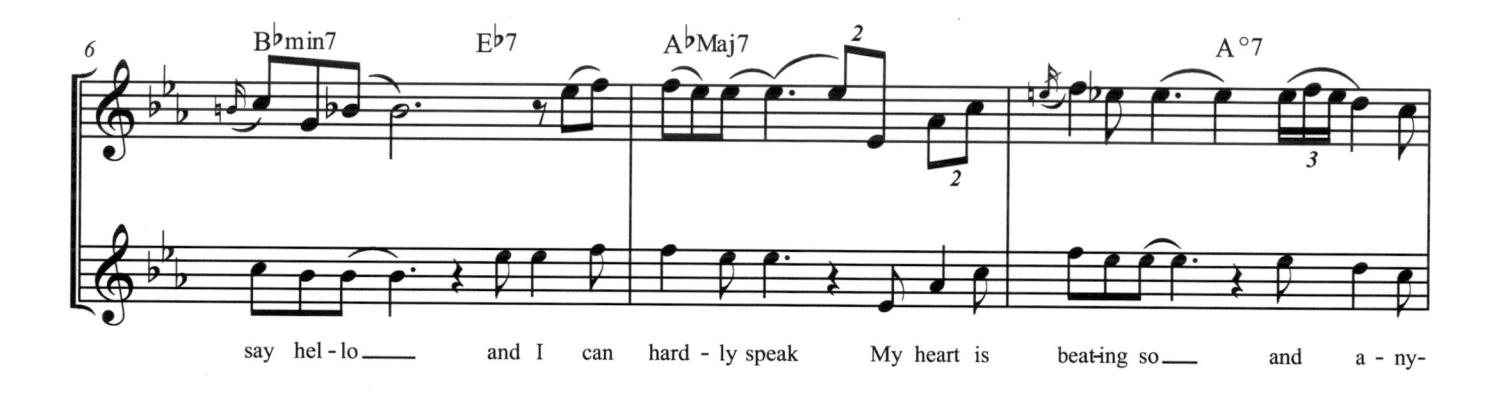

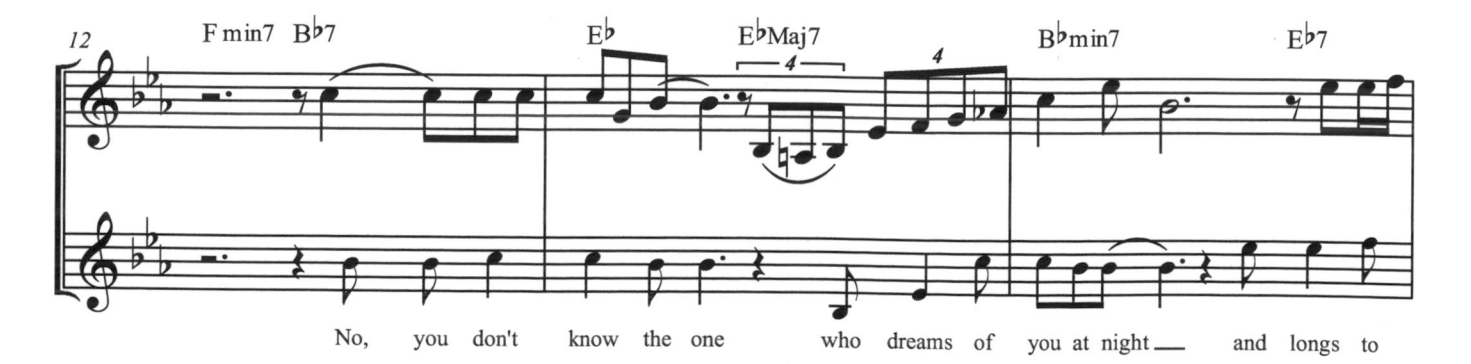

You Don't Know Me

kiss your lips and longs to hold you tight __ To you I'm just a friend that's all I've

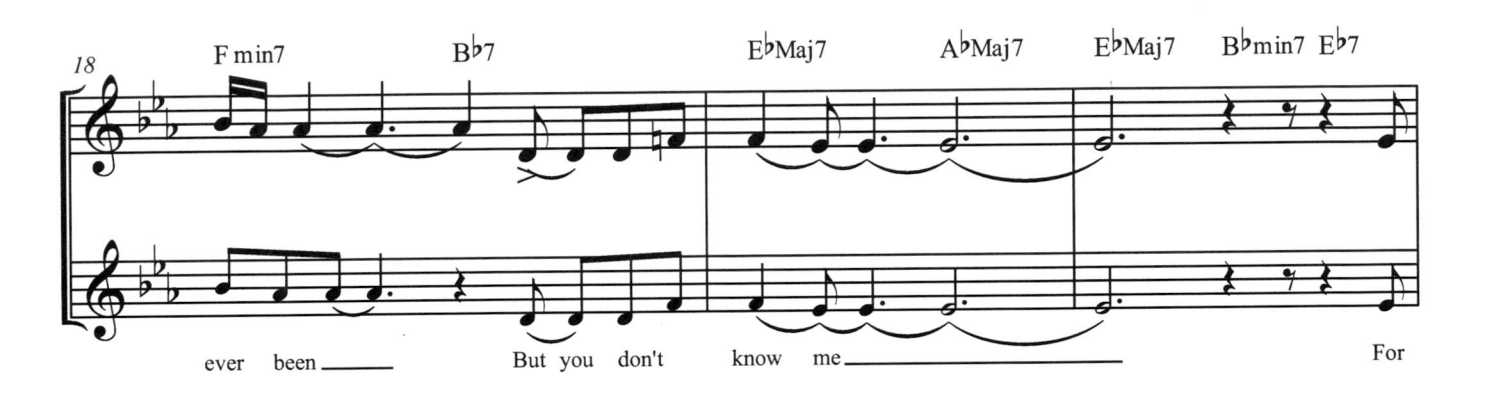

ever been ___ But you don't know me _____ For

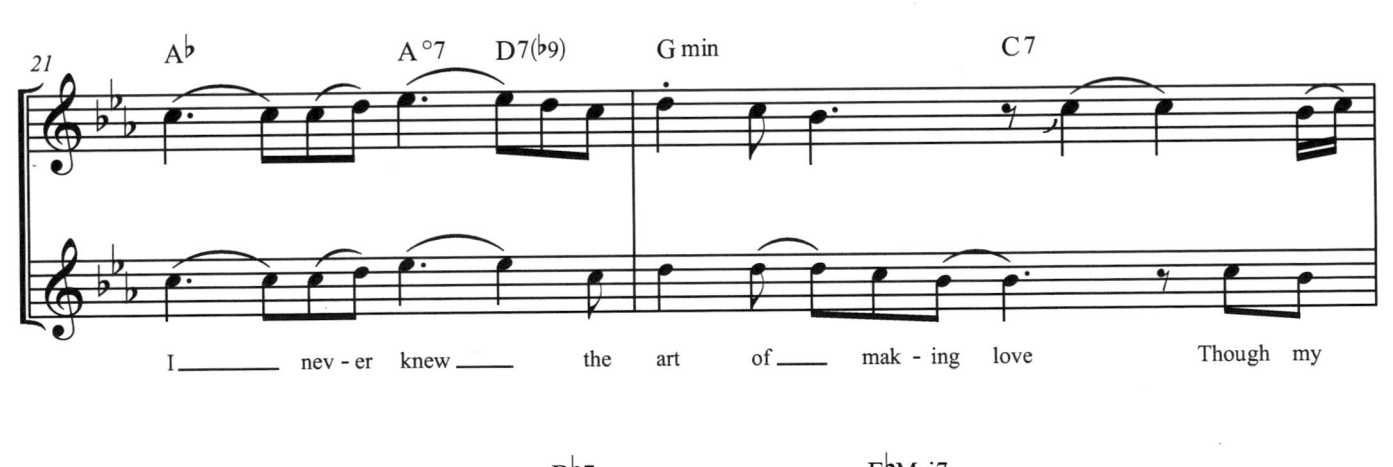

I_____ nev - er knew ___ the art of __ mak - ing love Though my

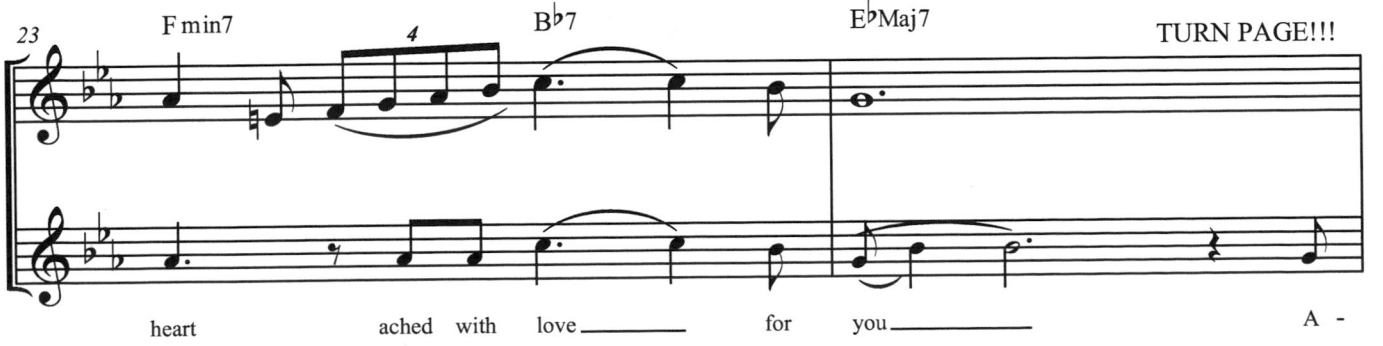

heart ached with love ___ for you _____ A -

You Don't Know Me

Transcribed and edited by Kevin Mauldin

This page intentionally left blank to facilitate page turns.

Solo Bb Trumpet

Steppin' Out With My Baby

Irving Berlin

MMO 6855

Transcribed by Jeff Helgesen

Solo Bb Flugelhorn

Days of Wine and Roses

Henry Mancini
Johnny Mercer

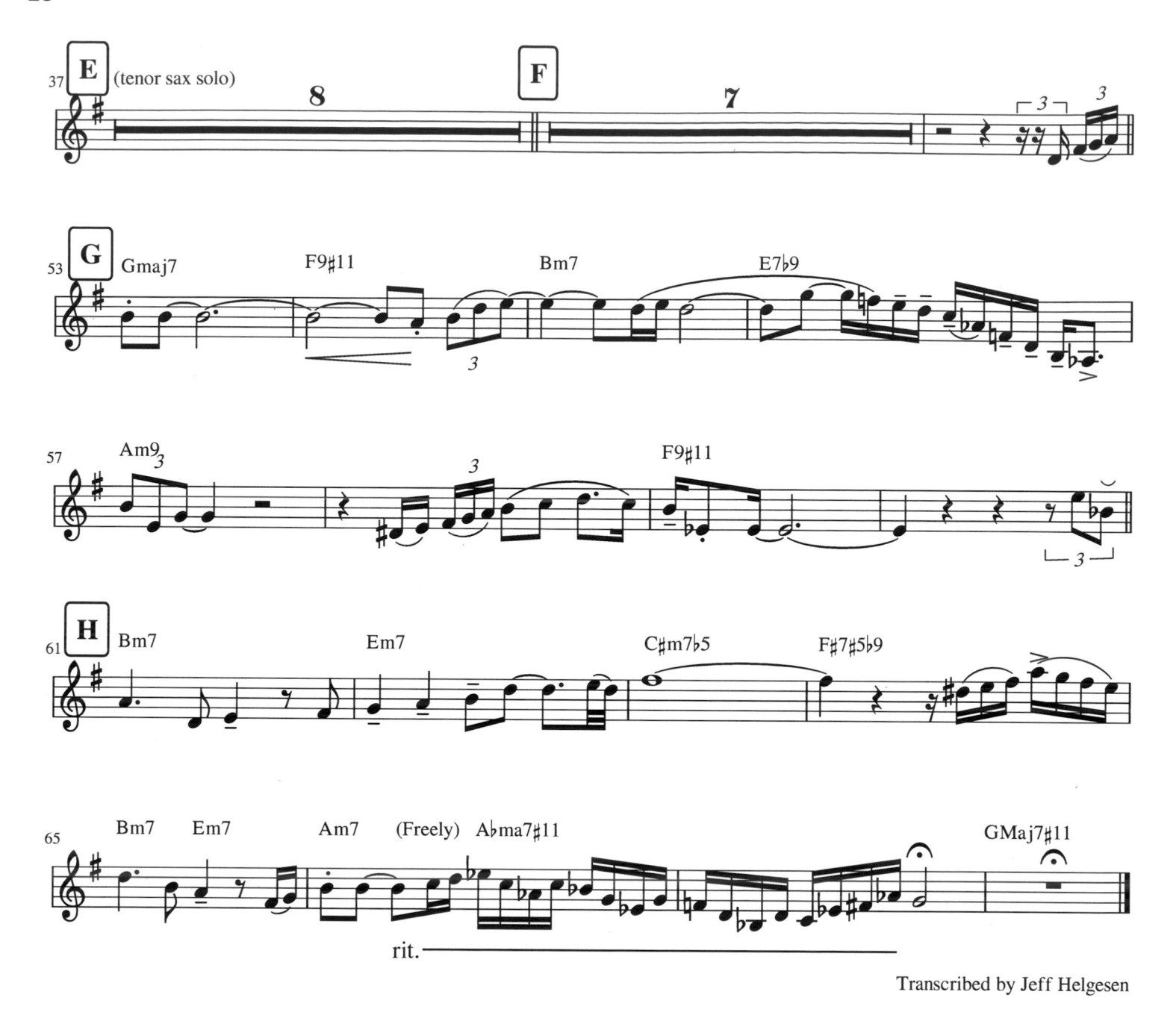

Transcribed by Jeff Helgesen

This page intentionally left blank to facilitate page turns.

Solo Bb Trumpet

God Bless The Child

Arthur Herzog, Jr.
Billie Holiday

MMO 6855

Transcribed by Jeff Helgesen

Music Minus One   50 Executive Boulevard • Elmsford, New York 10523-1325
914-592-1188 • e-mail: info@musicminusone.com
www.musicminusone.com

MMO 6855

ISBN 978-1-941566-96-1